Earth and Its Moon

HOUGHTON MIFFLIN

BOSTON

Photography and Illustration Credits
Front Cover Courtesy of NASA. **Title Page** © Darrell Gulin/Corbis.
1 © MPI/Getty Images. **2-3** © HMCo./Coppola Studios Inc. **4** Slim Films.
5 Slim Films. **6-7** Slim Films. **8** © Darrell Gulin/Corbis. **9** © MPI/Getty Images. **10** Courtesy of NASA/SOHO/EITD. **11** (illustration) Slim Films. (moon cycle photos) © Larry Landolfi/Photo Researchers, Inc.
12 (t) Slim Films. **(b)** © Roger Ressmeyer/Corbis. **13 (t)** Slim Films.
(b) © John Chumack/Photo Researchers, Inc. **14** Slim Films. **15** Slim Films.
Back Cover Slim Films.

Number of Words: 1,484

Copyright © by Houghton Mifflin Company. All rights reserved.

No part of this work may be reproduced or transmitted in any form or by any means, electronic or mechanical, including photocopying or recording, or by any information storage or retrieval system without the prior written permission of Houghton Mifflin Company unless such copying is expressly permitted by federal copyright law. Address inquiries to School Permissions, Houghton Mifflin Company, 222 Berkeley Street, Boston, MA 02116.

Printed in China

ISBN-13: 978-0-618-75983-5
ISBN-10: 0-618-75983-2

123456789-NPC-12 11 10 09 08 07 06

Contents

1 What Causes Earth's Seasons? 2

2 Why Does the Moon Have Phases? 8

Glossary 15

Responding 17

1 What Causes Earth's Seasons?

Earth rotates on its axis, causing day and night. Earth revolves around the Sun, causing the seasons.

Earth's Tilted Axis

Earth always rotates, or spins around. It rotates around an imaginary line called an **axis**. The axis is like a line that goes from the North Pole through the center of Earth to the South Pole. This line is not straight up and down. It is tilted at an angle of 23 ½ degrees.

It takes 23 hours and 56 minutes for Earth to rotate once around. This time period is called a day. As Earth rotates, different parts face the Sun. The side of Earth facing the Sun has daytime. The side facing away from the Sun has nighttime.

Sun and Earth in June

Summer in the Northern Hemisphere

Winter in the Southern Hemisphere

Earth's tilt causes the seasons.

Earth also moves around the Sun. One full trip around the Sun is called a **revolution**. It takes one year, or 365 ¼ days, to make one revolution.

Earth's axis is tilted. Some parts of Earth tilt toward the Sun during a revolution. Other parts tilt away from the Sun. The tilt causes the seasons.

It is summer when part of Earth tilts toward the Sun. It is winter when part of Earth tilts away from the Sun.

Study the photographs on pages 2 and 3. They show that when it is summer in the Northern Hemisphere, it is winter in the Southern Hemisphere.

Sun and Earth in December

Winter in the Northern Hemisphere

Summer in the Southern Hemisphere

Solstices and Equinoxes

In the Northern Hemisphere, the longest day of the year is June 21 or 22. On this day, the North Pole points *toward* the Sun. This is the **summer solstice** and marks the start of summer.

The shortest day of the year is the **winter solstice** on December 21 or 22. This marks the start of winter. On this day, the North Pole points directly *away* from the Sun.

There are two equinoxes each year. These are days when there is the same amount of sunlight and darkness everywhere on Earth. The **vernal equinox** is on March 21 or 22 and marks the start of spring. The **autumnal equinox** is on September 22 or 23 and marks the start of fall.

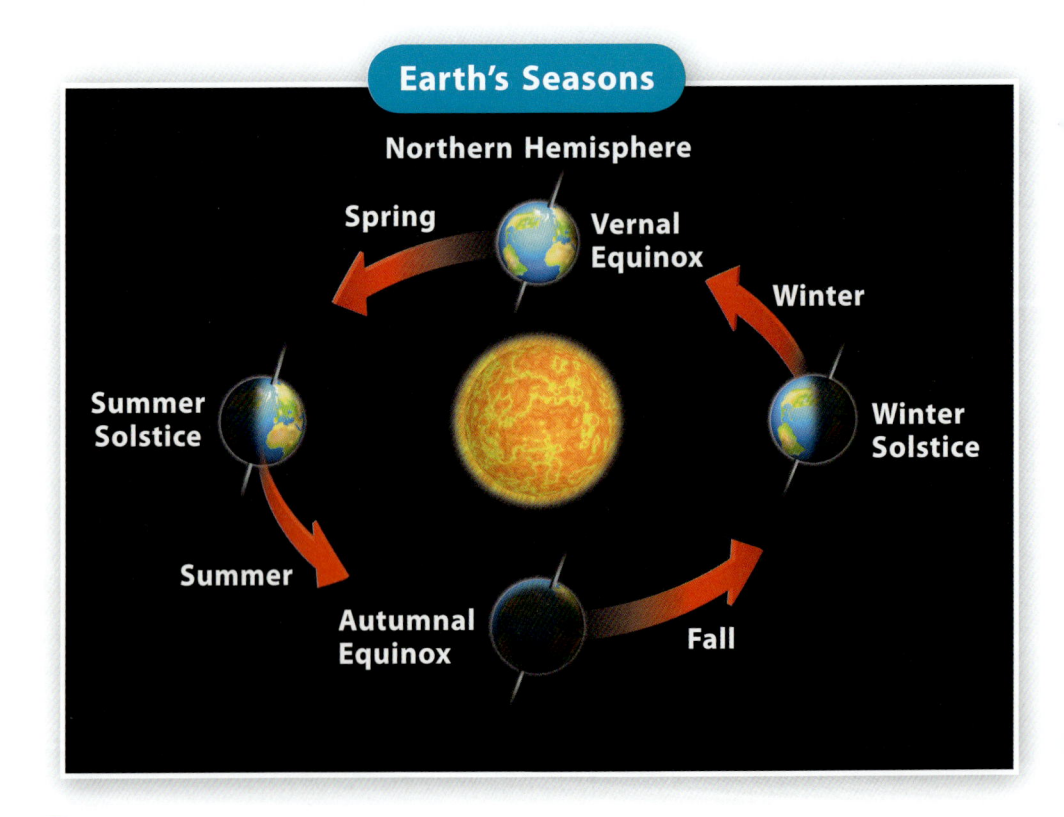

Earth's Seasons

Northern Hemisphere

- Spring — Vernal Equinox
- Summer Solstice — Summer
- Autumnal Equinox — Fall
- Winter Solstice — Winter

Seasons

All places on Earth have four seasons: spring, summer, fall, and winter. Not all places on Earth feel the seasons in the same way.

Near the poles, the Sun's rays hit at sharp angles. These places, such as McMurdo on the South Pole, have cold weather all year long. Near the equator, the Sun's rays hit more directly. These places, such as Panama City, have mostly warm weather.

Some places feel the seasons more strongly. Chicago, Illinois and Santiago, Chile are about halfway between the equator and a pole. Their temperatures go up and down a lot. This shows that a place's position on Earth has a big effect on the place's weather and seasons.

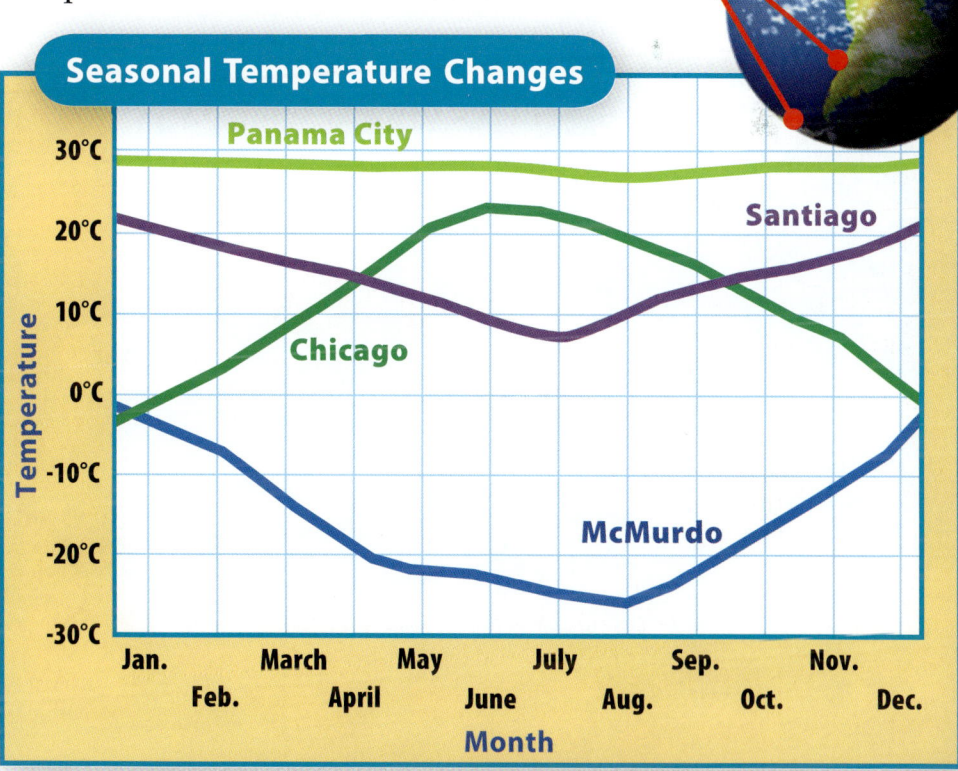

Seasonal Temperature Changes

An area's position on Earth affects the weather there.

Ideas About the Sun

Hundreds of years ago, people did not know much about the Sun. They had false ideas about it. That means that the thoughts they had about the Sun were actually wrong. For example, people used to think that Earth was the center of the universe. They thought the Sun revolved around Earth.

Galileo was an astronomer. An astronomer is a person who studies the skies. In the 1600s he wrote a book that said that Earth revolved around the Sun. He also explained why this happened. He was arrested for telling others about his idea.

Today, we know that Galileo was correct. Based on his work, scientists can tell where Earth, the Sun, and other objects will appear in the sky.

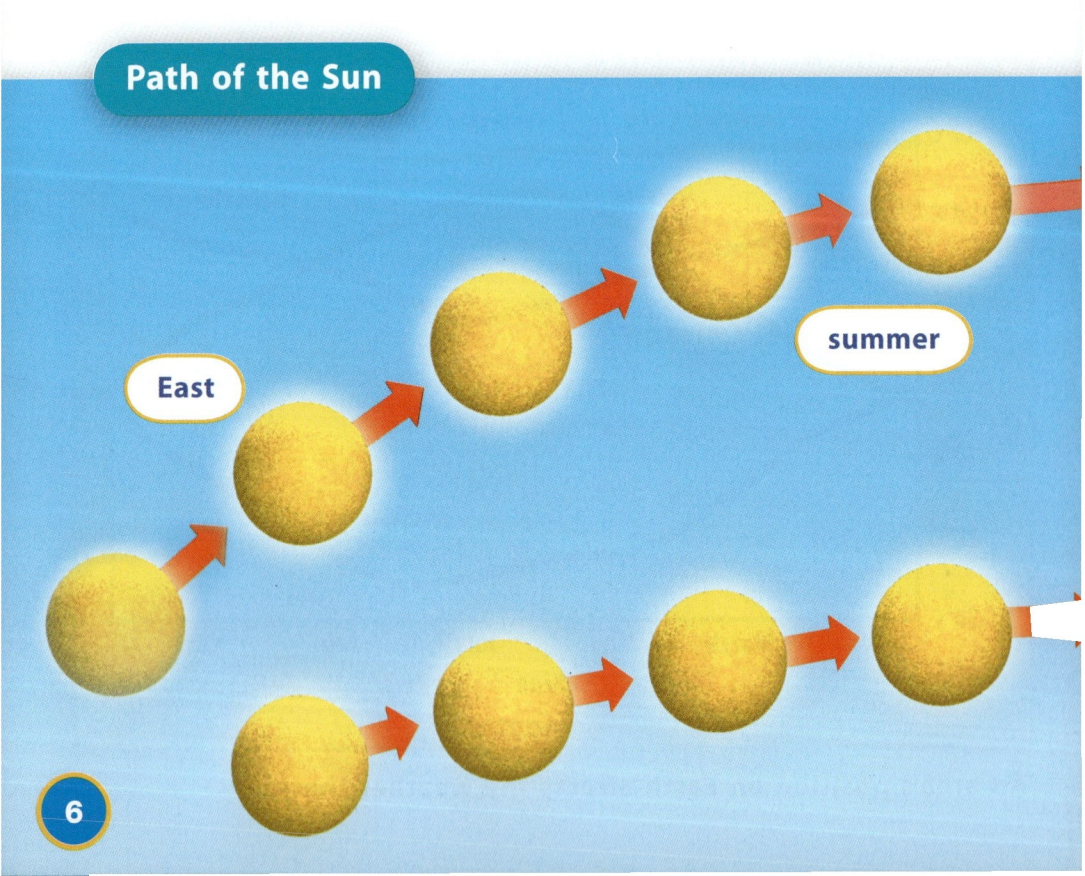

Path of the Sun

East

summer

People had other false ideas, too. They thought that the seasons came because of Earth's distance from the Sun. We now know that Earth is actually closer to the Sun in December than in June. We also know that the seasons are caused by Earth's tilted axis and revolutions around the Sun. Because of the tilt, the Sun rises higher in the sky. This makes summer days last longer.

Study the picture. It shows how the Sun seems to travel across the sky in the Northern Hemisphere. The Sun is higher in the summer, so the days are longer and warmer.

CAUSE AND EFFECT

Why do the Northern and Southern hemispheres have opposite seasons?

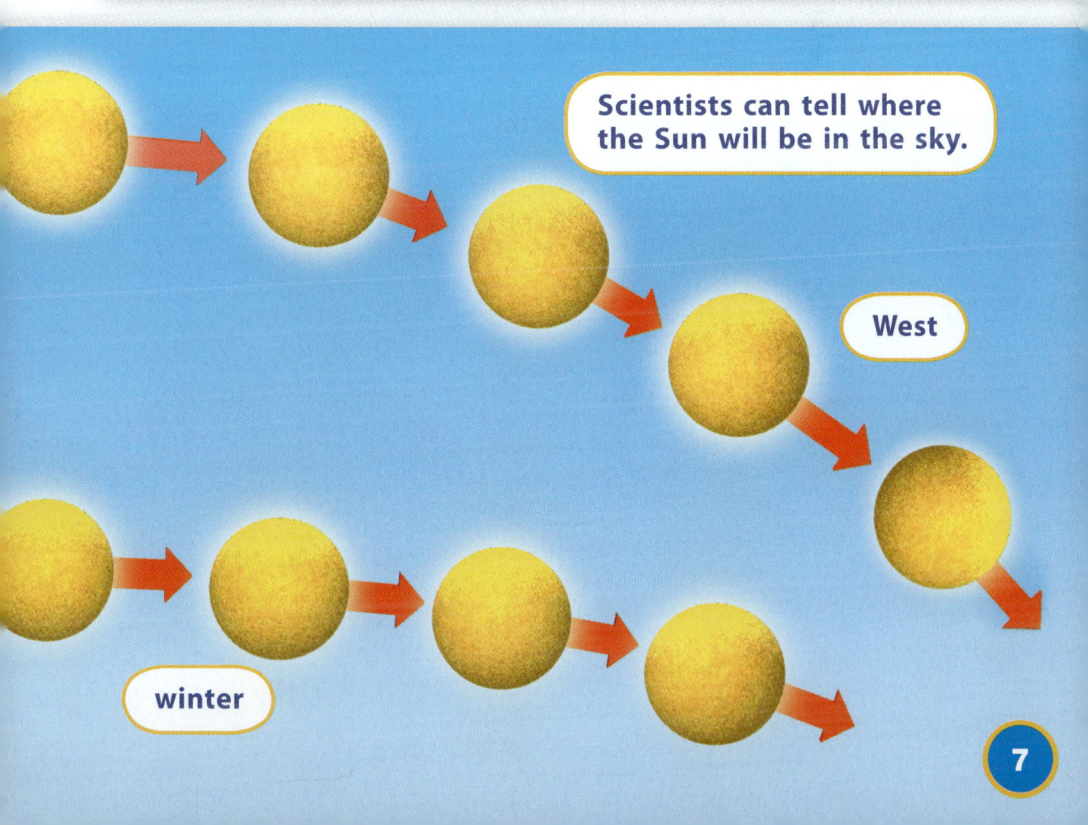

Scientists can tell where the Sun will be in the sky.

West

winter

2 Why Does the Moon Have Phases?

The Moon revolves around Earth, and they revolve around the Sun together. The same side of the Moon always faces Earth, but the Sun lights up different parts of the Moon at different times.

The Moon

A satellite is an object that revolves around Earth. The Moon is a satellite. It is Earth's only natural satellite.

The Moon is a sphere, or round like a ball. It is much smaller than Earth, and is 80 times lighter. Compared to Earth, the Moon does not have a very strong gravitational pull. Because of this, there is not much of an atmosphere around the Moon. Its gravity, though, is strong enough to affect Earth's tides.

The Moon revolves around Earth.

There are rocks on the surface of the Moon. They are about 4.6 billion years old.

Viewing the Moon

At night, the Moon seems to be the biggest and brightest object in the sky. It is really much smaller than the other objects, though. It just looks large because it is so close to Earth. The planet Venus is about the same size as Earth. It looks like a small dot in the sky. Because the Moon is closer to Earth, it looks much larger than Venus.

The Moon looks bright at night. However, it does not produce any light. It looks bright because the Sun is shining on it. That is why you can see the Moon from Earth.

Like Earth, the Moon rotates on an imaginary axis. One full rotation takes 27 $\frac{1}{3}$ days. The Moon also revolves, but around Earth, not the Sun. It takes 27 $\frac{1}{3}$ days for the Moon to revolve around Earth. As you can see, the Moon takes the same period of time to rotate and revolve. Because of this, the same side of the Moon always faces Earth.

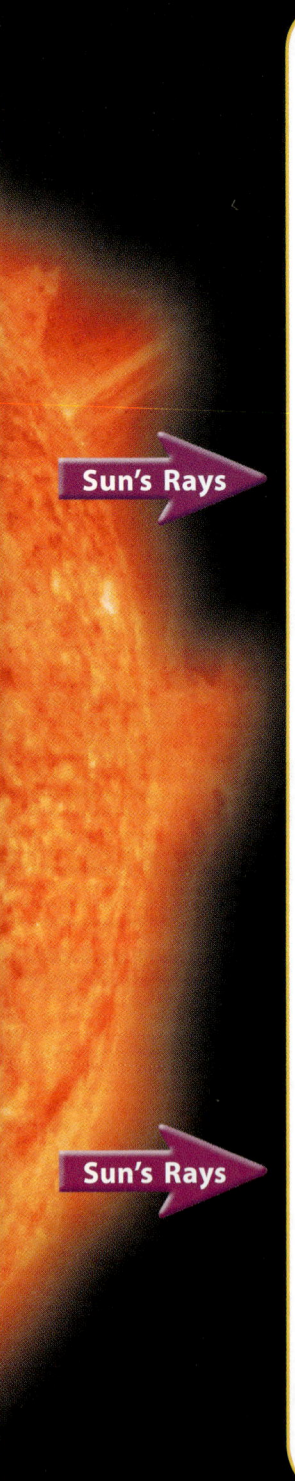

Phases of the Moon

The Sun is always shining on the Moon so one half of the Moon is always lit up. Because the Moon revolves around Earth, the entire lit up half is not visible. Only parts of the lighted half can be seen. The shapes created by the changing amounts of the visible lighted areas are called **Moon phases**. A complete cycle of the Moon phases takes about one month.

The first phase is the new Moon. In this phase, the Moon is between Earth and the Sun. The lit side of the Moon is facing away from Earth. So the Moon appears dark.

The Moon continues to revolve around Earth. Now more of the lit area can be seen. The next phase is called waxing crescent. The Moon appears to be waxing, or growing. Soon half of the lit area can be seen. Now the Moon is in its first quarter phase. More and more of the Moon is visible until the full Moon phase is reached. In this phase, the entire lit side can be seen.

The Moon then appears to be waning, or getting smaller. Less of the lit side can be seen. The phases at this point in the revolution are called waning gibbous, last quarter, and waning crescent.

Phases of the Moon

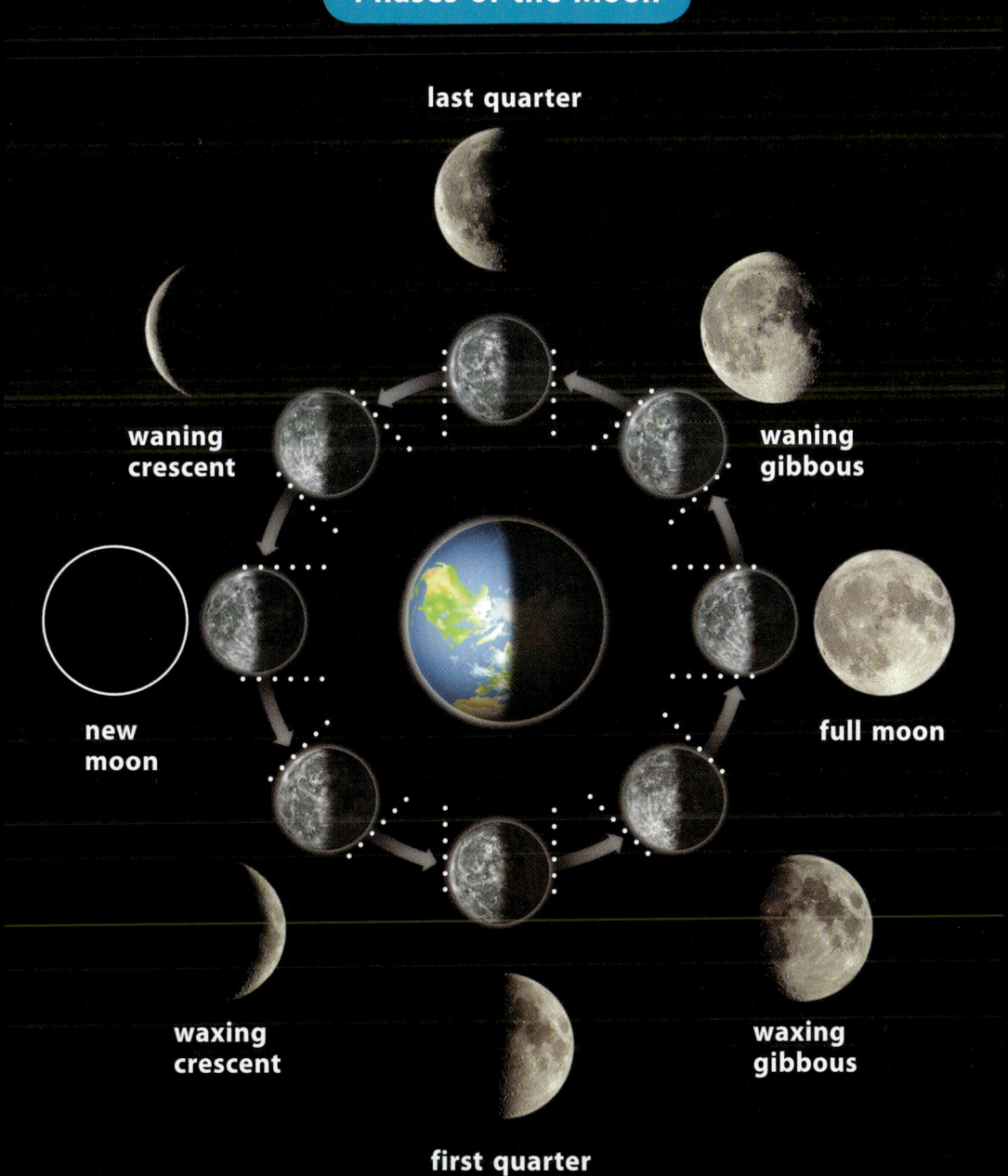

last quarter

waning crescent

waning gibbous

new moon

full moon

waxing crescent

waxing gibbous

first quarter

Eclipses

An eclipse is when one object passes into the shadow of another object. Sometimes Earth, the Sun, and the Moon are lined up in a straight line. This can form two kinds of eclipses.

A **solar eclipse** takes place when the Moon passes between the Sun and Earth. The Moon blocks the light from the Sun. This makes a shadow on Earth.

The shadow has two parts. One part is darker than the other. The darker part of the shadow is called the umbra. The parts of Earth in this area have a total solar eclipse. The lighter part of the shadow is the penumbra. The parts of Earth in this area have a partial solar eclipse.

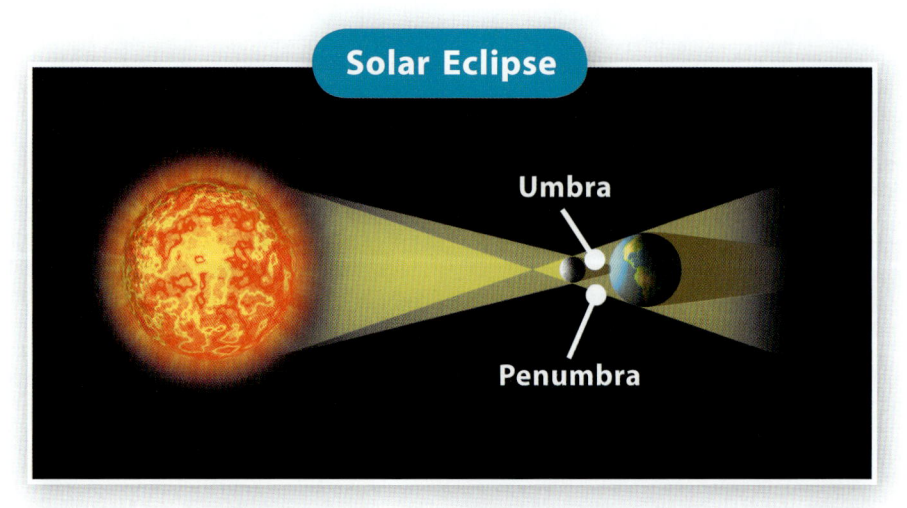

Solar Eclipse

Umbra

Penumbra

The Moon goes between the Sun and Earth.

A total solar eclipse

A **lunar eclipse** takes place when Earth passes directly between the Sun and the Moon. The Moon then moves into Earth's shadow.

A total lunar eclipse takes place when the entire Moon passes into the umbra, or darker part, of Earth's shadow. The Moon can still be seen during this time, but it looks different. It has a reddish color. During a partial lunar eclipse, only part of the Moon passes into the umbra. The rest of the Moon is in the penumbra.

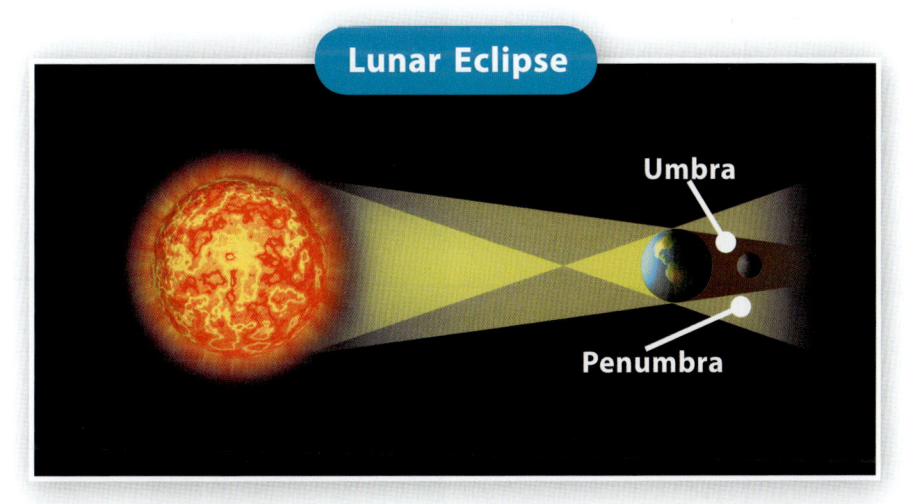

Lunar Eclipse

Umbra

Penumbra

Earth goes between the Sun and the Moon.

A total lunar eclipse

Moon Facts

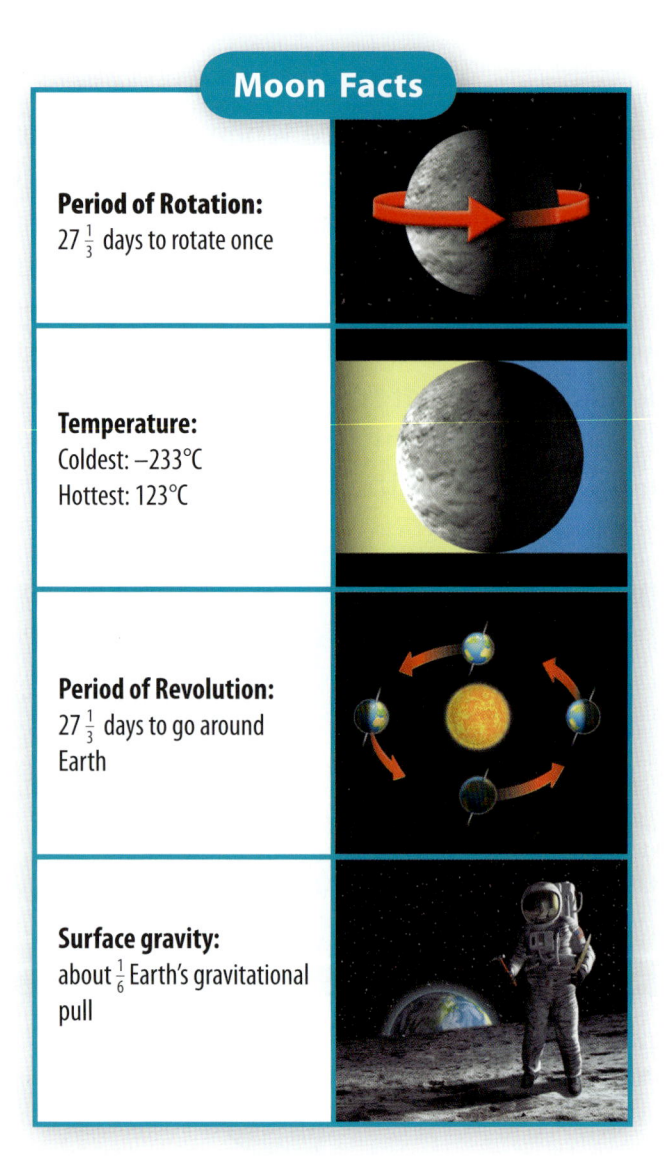

Period of Rotation: $27\frac{1}{3}$ days to rotate once	
Temperature: Coldest: −233°C Hottest: 123°C	
Period of Revolution: $27\frac{1}{3}$ days to go around Earth	
Surface gravity: about $\frac{1}{6}$ Earth's gravitational pull	

SEQUENCE

Why does the Moon go through phases?

Glossary

autumnal equinox (aw TUHM nuhl EE kwuh nahks), September 22 or 23, when the number of hours of daylight and darkness are the same

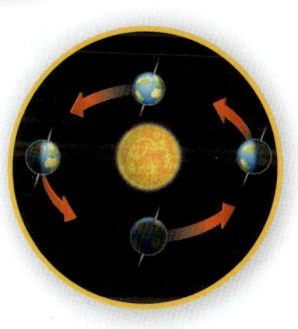

axis (AK sihs), imaginary line that goes through the center of Earth from the North Pole to the South Pole

lunar eclipse (LOO nuhr ih KLIHPS), when Earth passes directly between the Sun and the Moon, casting a shadow on the Moon

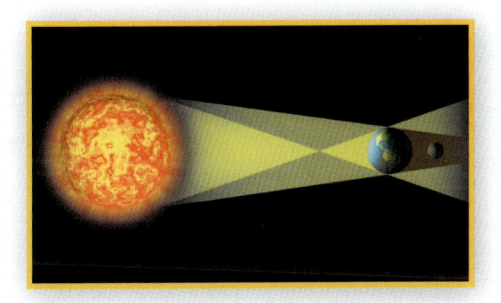

Moon phases (moon FAYZ ihz), shapes created by the changing amounts of the visible lighted areas of the Moon

revolution (rehv uh LOO shuhn), one full trip, or orbit, around the Sun

Glossary

solar eclipse (SOH luhr ih KLIHPS), when the Moon passes directly between the Sun and Earth, casting a shadow on Earth

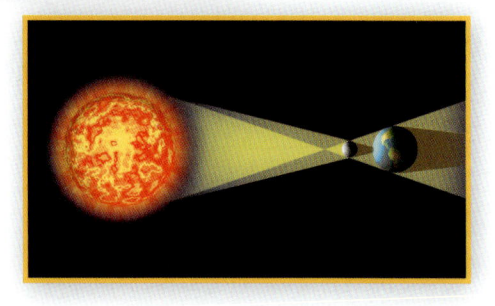

summer solstice (SUHM uhr SAHL stihs), June 21 or 22, the longest day of the year in the Northern Hemisphere

vernal equinox (VUR nuhl EE kwuh nahks), March 20 or 21, when the number of hours of daylight and darkness are the same

winter solstice (WIHN tuhr SAHL stihs), December 21 or 22, the shortest day of the year in the Northern Hemisphere

Responding

Think About What You Have Read

Vocabulary

1 What happens during a total solar eclipse?

A) The Moon blocks out all of the Sun.

B) The Sun blocks out all of the Moon.

C) The Moon blocks out part of the Sun.

D) The Sun blocks out part of the Moon.

Comprehension

2 Why is the same side of the Moon always visible from Earth?

3 What causes day and night? What causes seasons?

4 Why can you see the Moon from Earth?

Critical Thinking

5 Explain why the shortest day of the year in the Northern Hemisphere is on December 21 or 22. Where is this the longest day?